CONTENTS

4

I WANT TO KNOW...

How does my body work?

Helena Ramsay

**Illustrated by
Stuart Trotter**

First published in this edition in 2011 by
Evans Publishing Group
2A Portman Mansions
Chiltern Street
London W1U 6NR

© Evans Brothers Limited 2011

www.evansbooks.co.uk

British Library Cataloguing in Publication Data:
A CIP catalogue record for this book is available from the British Library

ISBN: 9780237544959

Planned and produced by Discovery Books
Cover designed by Rebecca Fox

For permission to reproduce copyright material the author and publishers gratefully acknowledge the following: Action Plus: page 25 (Mike Hewitt); Alex Ramsay: page 13; Image Bank: page 19 (Kahl Brandt); Istock: cover, page 15

Printed by Great Wall Printing Company in Chai Wan, Hong Kong, August 2011, Job Number 1672.

Food gives us the energy that we need to make our bodies work properly. When we do something very active, like swimming, we use lots of energy.

6

Your body needs the right kind of food to keep it healthy. It's important not to eat too many fatty or sugary foods, like chips and sweets.

When you are young, your body grows very quickly. When you are grown up, it stops growing.

There is an opening in your iris called the pupil. It looks like a black circle. In very bright light the pupil gets smaller, to stop too much light getting into your eye.

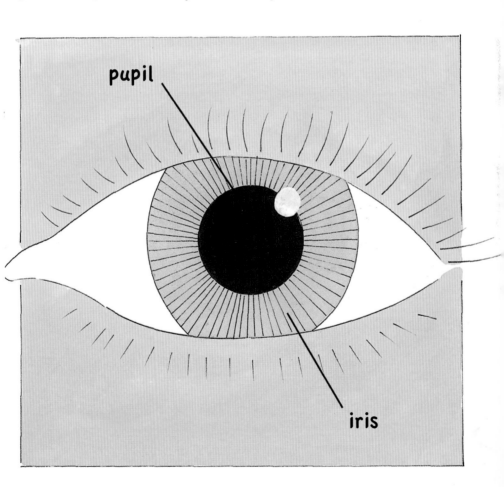

pupil

iris

When you start to run, the brain tells your heart to pump the blood around your body more quickly.

14

All the different parts of your body need oxygen to make them work. When you breathe, your lungs take in oxygen from the air. Then your blood carries the oxygen around your body.

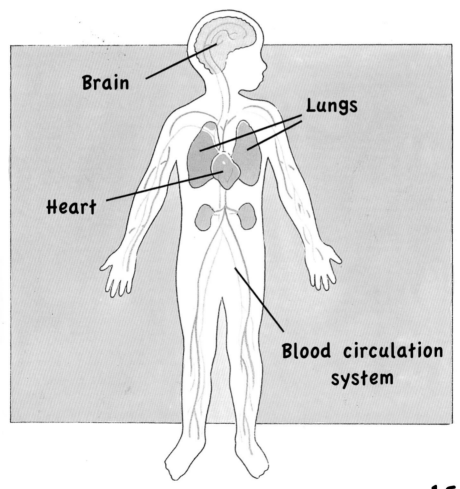

Brain

Lungs

Heart

Blood circulation system

Your muscles help you to move around. They work by expanding and contracting.

Your muscles are joined to your bones by cords called tendons. When they expand and contract, they move your bones with them.

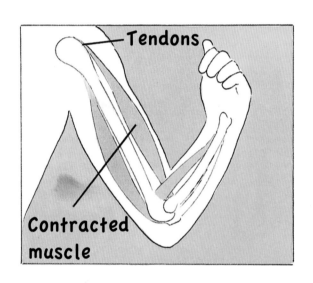

Tendons

Contracted muscle

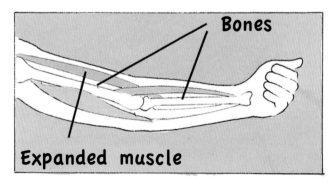

Bones

Expanded muscle

If you are running or swimming very fast, your muscles can get tired and run out of oxygen.

That is when you get a pain in your side. We call it a stitch.

You have to hold your breath when you swim under water.

When you get too cold, you can't help shivering. It's your body's way of warming you up. If you get too hot, your body sweats to cool you down.

28

That's because you've used up all the food you ate to make energy for your body.

Fun activities

Can you name these parts of the body? The answers are at the bottom of the page, but don't peep until you have tried yourself.

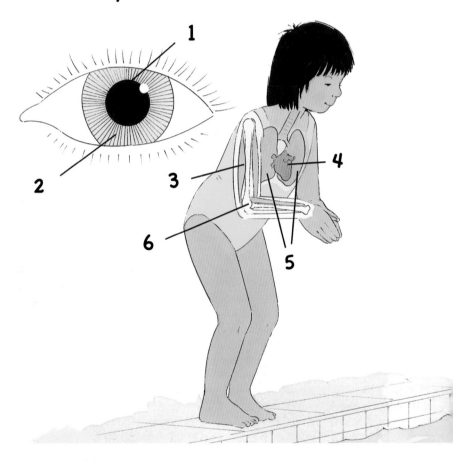

Create an energy chart

How does your body use energy during the day? Draw a table like the one below. Make two columns, one to show the food you eat to give you energy and the other to show how you used that energy.

MY ENERGY	
Where my energy came from	How I used the energy
Breakfast Scrambled egg on toast Orange juice **In the park** Bottle of water Banana	Walked to the park Played football Walked home

Imagine it's sports day

Write about how you feel as you line up for the final race. Think about the different parts of your body. How hard will they have to work? Imagine what it's like to cross the finish line as the winner!

Interesting websites:

Find out more about how your body works at:
http://kidshealth.org/kid/htbw

http://www.kidnetic.com has lots of ideas on how you can be fit and eat healthily.

There are games and quizzes that help you find out more about the human body and mind at:
http://www.bam.gov

Index